Primary Sources *of* American Symbols™

The Liberty Bell

Jennifer Silate

The Rosen Publishing Group's
PowerKids Press™
PRIMARY SOURCE

Published in 2006 by The Rosen Publishing Group, Inc.
29 East 21st Street, New York, NY 10010

Editor: Eric Fein
Book Design: Michael DeLisio
Photo Researcher: Amy Feinberg

Photo Credits: cover © Leif Skoogfors/Corbis; p. 4 (left) © The Historical Society of Pennsylvania/Bridgeman Art Library, (right); p.16 (right) The Historical Society of Pennsylvania; p. 6 (top) © Superstock, (bottom) Library of Congress Geography and Map Division; p. 8 Dover Pictorial Archive Series; p. 11 Picture Collection, The Branch Libraries, The New York Public Library, Astor, Lenox and Tilden Foundations, (inset) National Archives; p. 13 (top) Courtesy of the Liberty Bell Shrine Museum, Zion Reformed United Church of Christ, on loan from the Lehigh County Historical Society/Photo by Maura B. McConnell, (bottom) Courtesy of the Lehigh County Historical Society/ Photo by Maura B. McConnell; p. 15 (left) The Liberty Bell by Friends of Freedom, Boston, 1856. Anti-Slavery Society 1839-1858.Jon A. Lindseth Suffrage Collection. Courtesy of the Division of Rare and Manuscript Collections, Cornell University Library, (middle) © National Portrait Gallery, Smithsonian Institution/Art Resource, NY, (right) © Bettmann/Corbis; p. 16 (left) © Bequest of Mrs. Benjamin Ogle Tayloe; Collection of the Corcoran Gallery of Art/Corbis; p. 19 Library of Congress Prints and Photographs Division, (inset) © Hulton/Archive/Getty Images; p. 20 © AP/Wide World Photos, (inset) Courtesy of the Franklin D. Roosevelt Library

First Edition`

Library of Congress Cataloging-in-Publication Data

Silate, Jennifer.
    The Liberty Bell / Jennifer Silate.— 1st ed.
    p. cm. — (Primary sources of American symbols)
    Includes bibliographical references and index.
    Contents: A bell for Pennsylvania — The first crack — Try, try again
    — Ringing the bell — Hidden for the Revolution — The Liberty Bell —
    The mystery of the crack — The Liberty Bell tour — The bell today.
    ISBN 1-4042-2687-7 (lib. bdg.)
    1. Liberty Bell—Juvenile literature. 2. Philadelphia
    (Pa.)—Buildings, structures, etc.—Juvenile literature. [1. Liberty
    Bell.] I. Title. II. Silate, Jennifer. Primary sources of American
    symbols.

F158.8.I3S55 2006
974.8'11—dc22
                                    2003020110

Manufactured in the United States of America

Contents

William Penn (1644–1718) was a wealthy Englishman. In 1681, England's King Charles II gave Penn the land that would become Pennsylvania. The name Pennsylvania means Penn's woods. Penn set up a democratic form of government in Pennsylvania.

A Bell for Pennsylvania

The Liberty Bell is more than 200 years old. It is owned by the city of Philadelphia, Pennsylvania. Pennsylvania was one of America's first colonies. William Penn started Pennsylvania in 1681. In 1701, he helped write Pennsylvania's **charter**.

An **assembly** helped to run the colony. On November 1, 1751, the assembly sent a letter to Robert Charles, in England. Charles was Pennsylvania's **colonial agent**. He represented the colony's interests in England. The assembly wanted a bell to be made which would hang in the **steeple** of the **statehouse** in Philadelphia. Charles ordered a bell from the Whitechapel Foundry in England.

◀ *This letter was written by Isaac Norris on November 1, 1751. Norris was the speaker, or leader, of the assembly. In the letter, Norris asks Robert Charles to get the best workmen to make a bell and have it examined carefully before it is shipped to America.*

The First Crack

The bell arrived in Philadelphia around September 1, 1752. It was hung in the statehouse on March 10, 1753. On that day, the bell was rung once to check its sound. To everyone's shock, the bell cracked that first time it was struck! The cracked bell was given to John Pass and John Stow, local **foundry** workers. They melted it down and remade the bell. This new bell was hung in the statehouse on March 29, 1753. When the new bell was rung, however, no one liked the sound it made. The bell was taken down again. Pass and Stow tried to fix its sound. By June 1753, the bell was put up in the statehouse for a third time. This bell weighed about 2,080 pounds (943 kg) and was 3 feet (.914 m) tall.

This drawing of the Philadelphia State House was made in the 1750s. The statehouse would later become known as Independence Hall. The Declaration of Independence, the U.S. Constitution, and the design for the American flag were all agreed upon in the statehouse.

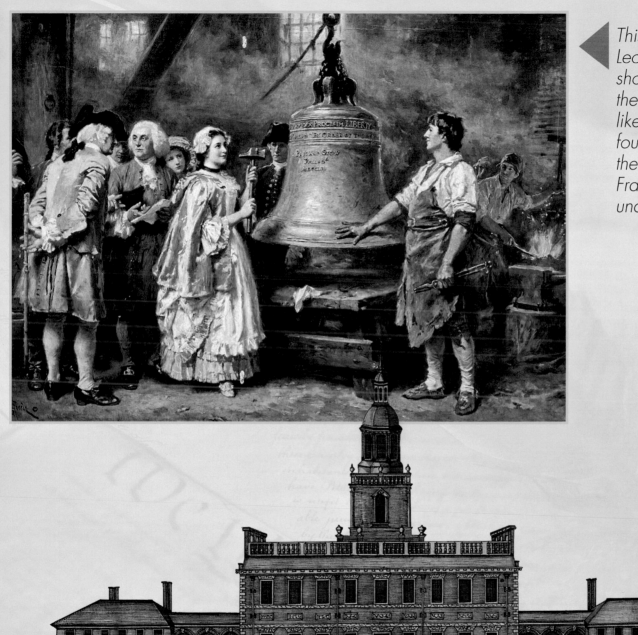

This painting by Jean Leone Gerome Ferris shows what the testing of the bell might have looked like at Pass and Stow's foundry. Included among the onlookers is Benjamin Franklin (holding his hat under his arm).

Try, Try Again

Not everyone was happy with Pass and Stow's second bell. Isaac Norris, speaker of the assembly, thought that the bell still did not sound right. Norris wrote to Robert Charles, asking that a new bell be made by the Whitechapel Foundry. When the new bell arrived in Philadelphia, its sound was tested. It did not sound any better than Pass and Stow's bell, which still hung in the statehouse steeple. It was decided that the new Whitechapel Foundry bell would be used as a clock bell. The Pass and Stow bell remained in the steeple. It is this bell that has come to be known as the Liberty Bell.

To make a bell, foundry workers had to make bell-shaped molds. Molten bronze was then poured in the space between the two molds. When it cooled, the molds were removed and the bell was created.

Ringing the Bell

   The Liberty Bell was used to call people to meetings. Many of these meetings were about the colonies' problems with England. England had placed high taxes on the goods that colonists used. The colonists refused to pay. England sent soldiers to America to force the colonists to follow England's laws. This angered the colonists and led to fighting between the two sides. On April 19, 1775, the **American Revolutionary War** began. The bell was rung to signal colonists that the war had started.

   On July 8, 1776, the bell rang to honor the first public reading of the **Declaration of Independence**. American colonel John Nixon read the Declaration of Independence to a crowd of people in Philadelphia. The Declaration of Independence stated that the people in Colonial America were free from England's rule.

This picture shows the signers of the Declaration of Independence leaving Philadelphia's statehouse after approving this document which announced the colonies' freedom from England.

The Declaration of Independence was written by Thomas Jefferson. John Adams, Benjamin Franklin, Robert Livingston, and Roger Sherman were chosen by the colonies' leaders to help Jefferson.

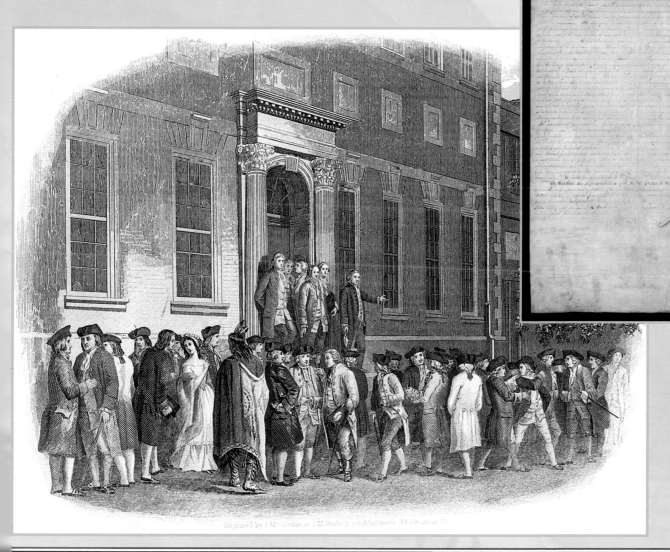

 This is a piece of the brake handle from the wagon that carried the Liberty Bell out of Philadelphia to a church in Allentown.

Dr. Jayne's
Indian Expectorant,

Wird empfohlen als die beste zubereitete Medizin für Huften, Erkältung, Auszehrung, Engbrüftig- keit, Keuchhuften, schweres Athmen und alle Krankheiten der Bruft und Lunge.

Diese Medizin wird von vielen und sehr respecta- beln Personen recommandirt, welche durch dieselbe cu- rirt wurden. Viele, welche lange Zeit unter Huften und Bruftkrankheiten litten und geglaubt haben sie wären mit der Auszehrung befallen, wurden in kur- zer Zeit gänzlich curirt und zur völligen Gesundheit gebracht.

Wer noch den Werth dieser Medizin bezweifelt, der lese den folgenden Brief von einer Person, die kein Interesse in dem Verkauf derselben hat:

New York, Juni 15, 1838

Nachricht.

Da David Laury von Nord-White- hall Taunschip, Lecha Caunty, vermittelft ei- ner freywilligen Ueberschreibung, datirt, den 2ten May 1840, all sein Eigenthum, sowohl liegendes als wie persönliches und vermischtes an Unterzeichnete übertragen hat, und zwar zum Besten seiner Crediteurs, so werden alle diejenigen, welche noch auf irgend eine Art diesenigen, welche noch auf irgend eine Art schuldig sind an besagten David Laury, aufge- fordert, unverzüglich zwischen jetzt und dem 1ften Juli a. J. Richtigkeit zu machen — und Solche, welche noch rechtmäßige Forderungen an ihn haben, belieben ihre Rechnungen eben- falls binnen besagtem Datum wohlbestätigt einzuhändigen, an

Daniel Säger,   } Affig-
James Neuhard.   } nies.

May 13.   nq — 6m

Stiefel- und Schuh-Stohr,
zum Schild des großen Stiefels
No. 4 Wilson's Gebäude in der Hamilton Straße, in Allentaun.

Hebräisches Pflaster.
Des Juden Davids oder Hebräisches Pflaster.

Ist zuerst in Palestina entdeckt worden und seit ei- nigen Jahren wegen seiner außerordentlichen Heil- kraft über ganz Europa und Amerika verbreitet; es ist in folgenden Krankheiten mit gutem Erfolge an- gewandt worden: Rheumatism, Pedgra, Kopf- schmerzen, Zahnschmerzen, Schmerzen in der Seite, Huften, Rücken und Gliedern, im Hals und andern Geschwülften, Beinfraß, gegen Bruft- und andere Fieber, ebenfalls im Magen- und Glieder-Schwäch- en, allen Gebrechen der Frauenzimmer, Nerven- schwäche, x. Wenn dieses Pflaster zwischen den Schultern aufgelegt wird so ist es ein unfehlbares Mittel gegen alle Verkältungen, Huften, Schweindt- sucht, Auszehrung, Leber- und Lungenkrankheiten x.

Ithica, (N. J.) Oct. 16, 1839.

Die neue Reformirte Kirche in Allentaun.

Hidden for the Revolution

In October 1777, British soldiers took over Philadelphia. Weeks before the soldiers had arrived, the people of Philadelphia moved the Liberty Bell to Allentown, Pennsylvania. In Allentown, the Liberty Bell was hidden under the floorboards of a church. The colonists did not want the British soldiers to find the bell. They were worried that the British soldiers would melt the bell down. The melted bell could then be used to make cannons. In 1778, colonists brought the bell back to Philadelphia. The American Revolutionary War ended in 1783. However, the bell was not put back in the statehouse until 1785. This delay was because the wooden steeple had become rotted. The steeple had to be rebuilt before the bell could be hung from it again.

This German-language newspaper from 1840 featured an article and picture of the Allentown church that was used to hide the Liberty Bell.

The Liberty Bell

The bell was not known as the Liberty Bell until the late 1830s. At about this time, people against **slavery** began using the bell as a **symbol** for their antislavery cause. In 1837, an antislavery newspaper called *Liberty* began publication. A picture of the bell was used in the newspaper. William Lloyd Garrison started another antislavery newspaper called the *Liberator*. In 1839, he printed a poem called "The Liberty Bell" in his paper. The poem was about the bell in Philadelphia. This was the first time that the bell in the Philadelphia State House was formally called the Liberty Bell.

The Liberty Bell was a magazine printed by the American Anti-Slavery Society. The magazine featured poems, editorials, and songs written by well-known people of the day.

William Lloyd Garrison (1805-1879) helped found the American Anti-Slavery Society. He was its president for 23 years.

William Lloyd Garrison began publishing the *Liberator* in 1831. This issue is from April 23, 1831. *The Liberator's* saying was Our Country Is the World—Our Countrymen Are Mankind.

George Washington (1732–1799) led America's colonial army to victory against the British during the American Revolutionary War. He later played an important role in the formation of the U.S. government and was the first president of the United States.

PUBLIC LEDGER

AND DAILY TRANSCRIPT.

PHILADELPHIA, THURSDAY, FEB. 26.

ADVERTISING CITY LETTERS.—We perceive that the Public Ledger and Spirit of the Times continue to be the selected mediums in which the Letters remaining in the city post-office are advertised. We presume their subscription lists entitle them to this patronage, agreeably to the act of Congress. We are satisfied, so far as the Ledger is concerned, that such is the case. An inspection of the books, exhibited to us by the proprietors a few days ago, in which is entered a statement of each day's circulation for perhaps a year past, shows the actual number of copies struck off daily to range from 24,000 to 25,500. This is an immense edition for a daily paper, and it can be sustained (for no one supposes that the price at which the paper is afforded pays anything like the expense) only by the extensive advertising custom which it has constantly enjoyed.—Germantown Telegraph.

We took occasion while the Editor of the Telegraph was in town, a few days since, to ask him to make an examination of our packer's book, that he might satisfy himself that the Telegraph had done us injustice, in sneering, as it did a short time ago, at the idea that any daily paper could have such a circulation as had been rendered by us to the Postmaster of this city, under the provisions of the new post-office law, which requires the list of letters to be published in the paper or papers having the largest circulation. We called the attention of the editor of the Telegraph to this subject, with full confidence that, upon being satisfied of the facts of the case, he would correct any misimpression which his readers might have derived from his former remarks, which remarks were founded upon his own doubts. He has done so candidly and frankly; and is entitled to the credit of desiring to give his readers the facts. It would be well for themselves if all the publishers of news-

A MACHINE TO TEACH THE BLIND TO WRITE. —A machine by which the blind may be taught to write with the same facility as those who can see, has been invented. The instrument is said to be, in appearance, precisely like a small piano, or parlor organ. Each key is marked, (raised letters, if necessary, for the blind.) The keys are struck by the fingers precisely as in playing on the piano forte, and a small pen with common ink makes a letter at each touch of a note with the finger, on a sheet of paper fixed up in front of the instrument. The inventor is Charles Thurbur, Esq., of Norwich, Connecticut, a graduate of Brown University.

RESUMPTION OF STATE FAITH IN MARYLAND. A bill was presented in the Maryland Legislature on Tuesday, introduced by Mr. Johnson, for the funding of the arrears of interest on the State debt up to 1st of July next, and the resumption of the payment of interest accruing thereon on the 1st of October ensuing. The arrears of interest funded are to be at five per cent. per annum. This is truly the most important bill of the session.

A CHALLENGE.—Some difficulty existing between John Swan, Esq., a Delegate from Allegheny, Md., and Thomas McKaig, Esq., of the same county, they proceeded to the neutral ground, at Bladensburg, on Monday morning last, where the matter was amicably and honorably settled, by the mutual interference of friends.

BRITISH VESSELS OF WAR FOR OREGON.—The London Morning Chronicle of the 26th January states: "It is reported that her Majesty's ship America, 50, Commodore the Hon. John Gordon, with a steamship and a brig, had been despatched by Rear-Admiral Sir George Seymour, to the Columbia river, on the Oregon; and the Grampus, 50, is expected to be sent thither when her magazine is altered."

THE OREGON CORRESPONDENCE has been printed in German at Bremen, and upon the

A Shocking Spectacle.—As a number of gentlemen were returning from a funeral yesterday, in the southwestern part of the city, their attention was called to an enclosed lot on the south side of Carpenter street, near Seventh, by a crowd of persons, and on looking over the fence discovered the attraction to be a large number of hogs feeding upon a horse. We do not wish to spoil the breakfast of those who may be addicted to sausages, or Jersey hams, but we cannot refrain from pronouncing such an exhibition positively shocking. Our informant assures us that the spectacle was not an accidental one, as the hogs were confined within the enclosure, and the carrion had evidently been carried to them. We are also informed from another quarter that the disgusting practice here referred to is not an uncommon one in the country, and that a large amount of the pork sold in the city for genuine "corn fed" is manufactured in this way. If so, some police regulation should be made to stop such a shocking practice for the future, if the present laws are not sufficient to prevent and punish it.

The Old Independence Bell.—This venerable relic of the Revolution rang its last clear note on Monday last, in honor of the birth day of Washington, and now hangs in the great city steeple irreparably cracked and forever dumb. It had been cracked long before, but was put in order for that day, by having the edges of the fracture filed so as not to vibrate against each other, as there was a prospect that the church bells would not chime upon that occasion. It gave out clear notes and loud, and appeared to be in excellent condition until noon, when it received a sort of compound fracture in a zig-zag direction through one of its sides, which put it completely out of tune and left it a mere wreck of what it was. We were lucky enough to get a small fragment of it and shall keep it sacred, in memory of the good and glory achieved by the old herald of Independence in times long past, and ever to be remembered. It has been suggested that the bell should be recast; and, as it is now entirely useless, but composed of "good stuff," the suggestion is entitled to consideration. It can never be replaced but by itself, and although it may not be improved, yet, pure as it is, it can be re-formed to much advantage.

Railroad Accident.—Daniel I. Herrington, aged 23, had his left arm fractured on Tuesday evening, by being jammed between two cars

The Mystery of the Crack

Just like the first Whitechapel Foundry bell, the Liberty Bell has a large crack in it. The crack is 24 ½ inches (62.2 cm) long and ½ inch (1.3 cm) wide. No one knows for certain when the first crack was made. There are several stories about how the bell cracked. One story dates back to 1835. It is said that the bell cracked after several boys were allowed to ring the bell in honor of George Washington's birthday. Neither this or any other story can be proven true. What *is* known is that the crack appeared in the bell by 1846. Records show that there was a crack in the bell at that time but that it had been fixed. The bell was rung on Washington's birthday that year. Soon after that ringing, a large crack appeared in the bell.

◄ *This page of the Philadelphia newspaper the* Public Ledger *is from February 26, 1846. The light gray section in the lower righthand corner contains an article about the Liberty Bell being rung in honor of Washington's birthday.*

The Liberty Bell Tour

The Liberty Bell became a very popular symbol in America. In 1847, a Pennsylvania writer named George Lippard wrote a story about the day the Liberty Bell was rung to celebrate the Declaration of Independence. Americans loved the story and wanted to see the famous bell for themselves. In 1852, the Liberty Bell was taken down from the steeple and placed inside the statehouse.

Between 1876 and 1915, the Liberty Bell was taken all over the country. The bell traveled over 10,000 miles (16,000 km) on its way from Philadelphia to San Francisco, California. At first, Philadelphia officials did not want the cracked bell to go on this trip. However, letters from hundreds of thousands of schoolchildren changed the officials' minds.

This 1903 photo shows the Liberty Bell while it was on tour. At many places along its trip, there was a party to honor the bell.

In 1893, the bell was on display at the World's Columbian Exposition, in Chicago, Illinois. It honored the 400th anniversary of Christopher Columbus' discovery of America.

In October 2003, the Liberty Bell was moved into its new location in the Liberty Bell Center. The center is located in the Independence National Historical Park in Philadelphia. The Philadelphia statehouse, now called Independence Hall, can be seen in the background.

The Bell Today

The Liberty Bell is no longer rung. People fear ringing the bell will cause it to crack further. Sometimes, it is allowed to be lightly tapped for special celebrations. The Liberty Bell has been tapped several times over the years. In 1926, it was tapped to mark the 150th **anniversary** of America's **independence**. During World War II, the bell was tapped on June 6, 1944. On this day, D-Day, American forces landed in France.

On America's **bicentennial** in 1976, the bell was moved to an area near the statehouse, which is now called Independence Hall. In 2003, the bell was moved to the Liberty Bell Center. About 1,500,000 people visit the Liberty Bell each year. The Liberty Bell is a symbol of how highly Americans value their freedom and **liberty**.

The landing of American forces on the beaches of northern France was a turning point in World War II. Soldiers had to walk through water and dodge enemy fire as they made their way to the beaches.

Timeline

1681	William Penn starts the colony of Pennsylvania.
1701	The charter of Pennsylvania is written.
1751	Pennsylvania's assembly sends a letter to Robert Charles asking for a bell to be made for their statehouse.
1752	Whitechapel Foundry's bell arrives in Philadelphia.
March 10, 1753	The bell cracks on its first ringing.
March 29, 1753	Pass and Stow's first bell is hung.
June, 1753	Pass and Stow's second bell is hung.
1775–1783	The American Revolutionary War is fought.
July 8, 1776	Colonel John Nixon reads Declaration of Independence; Liberty Bell is rung.
October 1777	British troops invade Philadelphia. The Liberty Bell is hidden in an Allentown church.
1785	The Liberty Bell is put up in statehouse steeple again.
1839	"Liberty Bell" appears in William Lloyd Garrison's newspaper, the *Liberator*. It is the first known use of Liberty Bell as the bell's name.
1852	The Liberty Bell is taken down from statehouse steeple.
1915	The Liberty Bell ends its 39-year tour of the United States.
1926	The Liberty Bell is tapped for 150th anniversary of America's independence.
2003	Liberty Bell Center becomes the new home of the Liberty Bell.

Glossary

American Revolutionary War (uh-MER-uh-kuhn rev-uh-LOO-shuh-ner-ee WOR) The war from 1775–1783 during which the American colonies fought against England. As a result, the United States of America was created.

anniversary (an-uh-VUR-suh-ree) A date that people remember because something important happened on that date in the past.

assembly (uh-SEM-blee) A group of people who make laws for others.

bicentennial (BI-sen-ten-ee-uhl) The honoring of a 200th anniversary.

charter (CHAR-tur) A formal document that states the rights or duties of a group of people.

colonial agent (kuh-LOH-nee-uhl AY-jent) Someone who represented the members of a colony to England.

Declaration of Independence (dehk-luh-RAY-shuhn UHV in-dih-PEN-duhnss) A document declaring the freedom of American colonies from England.

foundry (FOUN-dree) A factory for melting and shaping metal.

independence (in-di-PEN-duhnss) Being free.

liberty (LIB-ur-tee) Freedom.

slavery (SLAYV-uh-ree) The practice of owning other people.

statehouse (STAYT-houss) The state capitol building.

steeple (STEE-puhl) A high tower on a building.

symbol (SIM-buhl) A design or an object that represents something else.

Index

Primary Sources

Cover: Liberty Bell [1990]. Photograph of the bell by Leif Skoogfors. **Page 4 (left):** Portrait of William Penn [c.1700s]. Pastel on paper by Francis Place. The Historical Society of Pennsylvania. **Page 4:** A letter written by Isaac Norris [November 1, 175 The Historical Society of Pennsylvania. **Page 7 (top):** Philadelphia's Liberty Bell bein tested in the Pass and Stow Foundry. [c. late 1800s/early 1900s]. Painting by Jea Leon Gerome Ferris. **Page 7:** The statehouse. [c.1752] A drawing taken from a m by George Heap. Library of Congress. **Page 8:** Casting Bells I. [c.1700s.] Black white plate. Artist unknown. *A Diderot Pictorial Encyclopedia of Trades and Industr* Printed in Paris, France. **Page 11:** The Announcement of the Declaration of Independence, State House, Philadelphia. [c. 1860]. An engraving by John McG Picture Collection, The Branch Libraries, The New York Public Library, Astor, Lenox Tilden Foundations. **Page 11 (inset):** The Declaration of Independence [1776]. The official, signed Declaration of Independence. National Archives. **Page 12 (top):** P brake handle from the wagon that carried the Liberty Bell. [c.1700s]. Photograph. Liberty Bell Shrine Museum, Zion Reformed United Church of Christ, on loan from t Lehigh County Historical Society. **Page 12 (bottom):** Front page of the June 3, 184 *Unabhaengiger Rupublikaner*. [1840]. The Lehigh County Historical Society. **Page (left):** *The Liberty Bell* by Friends of Freedom [1856]. Anti-Slavery Society Publicati Jon A. Lindseth Suffrage Collection. The Division of Rare and Manuscript Collection Cornell University Library. **Page 15 (center):** William Lloyd Garrison [c. early 1855 Painting by unknown artist. National Portrait Gallery, Smithsonian Institution. **Page (lower right):** Front page of the *Liberator* [April 23, 1831]. **Page 16 (left):** *George Washington* [c. 1796]. Painting by Gilbert Stuart. Bequest of Mrs. Benjamin Ogle Tayloe; Collection of the Corcoran Gallery of Art. **Page 16:** The *Public Ledger* [Fe 26, 1846]. The Old Independence Bell article. The Historical Society of Pennsylv **Page 19:** Liberty Bell being moved on a wagon with an escort of uniformed militi [c. 1903]. Photographic print. Library of Congress Prints and Photographs Division **Page 19 (inset):** Proclaim Liberty. [1893]. Color illustration. **Page 20:** Liberty Bell display at the Liberty Bell Center [October 10, 2003]. Photograph. AP/Wide W Photos. **Page 20 (inset):** WWII: Europe: France; "Into Jaws of Death—U.S. Troop wading through water and Nazi gunfire." [June 6, 1944]. Black and white photo Franklin D. Roosevelt Library.

Web Sites

Due to the changing nature of Internet links, PowerKids Press has developed an on-line list of Web sites related to the subject of this book. This site is updated regularly. Please use this link to access the list:
http://www.powerkidslinks.com/psas/tlb/